M000274685

MARILYN MONROE
IN · HER · OWN · WORDS

A DELILAH/PUTNAM BOOK
NEW YORK

ART DIRECTION BY MIKE BELL
BOOK DESIGNED BY BOB HOOK
PICTURE RESEARCH BY
    VALERIE BOYD
TYPESET BY CAPITAL LETTERS

DISTRIBUTED BY
THE PUTNAM PUBLISHING GROUP,
200 MADISON AVENUE,
NEW YORK,
NEW YORK 10016, USA.

© COPYRIGHT 1983 BY
OMNIBUS PRESS
(A DIVISION OF BOOK SALES LIMITED)

ISBN 0-399-41014-7

PICTURE CREDITS: JOEL FINLER
COLLECTION, THE RONALD GRANT
ARCHIVE, KOBAL COLLECTION, LONDON
FEATURES INTERNATIONAL,
PICTORIAL PRESS.

ALL RIGHTS RESERVED. NO PART OF
THIS BOOK MAY BE REPRODUCED IN
ANY FORM OR BY ANY ELECTRONIC OR
MECHANICAL MEANS, INCLUDING
INFORMATION STORAGE OR RETRIEVAL
SYSTEMS, WITHOUT PERMISSION IN
WRITING FROM THE PUBLISHER,
EXCEPT BY A REVIEWER WHO MAY
QUOTE BRIEF PASSAGES.

PRINTED IN THE UNITED STATES OF
AMERICA.

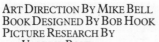

Marilyn Monroe [signature]

IN · HER · OWN · WORDS

CONTENTS

INTRODUCTION

Many words have been written and spoken about Marilyn Monroe. Her maids, her lovers, her directors and husbands have all had something to say about the "world's greatest sex symbol". By now, of course, such descriptions have become little more than clichés and one must continue to seek the truth behind the empty catch-phrases. In the case of this beautiful and remarkable woman, do they describe the multiple personalities and complexities of the simple country girl called Norma Jean who became known to the world as Marilyn Monroe – Love Goddess? Trying in vain to do so, countless books have been written, revealing (sometimes in lurid detail) different features of her life, her relation-ships with friends, lovers and colleagues – and often by people who never met her, let alone knew her.

It is exactly what she hoped would not happen. After reading a film script that had been prepared for *The Jean Harlow Story*, she said "I hope they don't do that to me after I'm gone". But they did, and will probably continue to do so. To an interviewer she once pleaded, "Don't make me a joke, end the interview with what I believe – I don't mind making jokes, but I don't want to look like one".

It seemed that all her life Marilyn was trying to prove to people that she wasn't just a joke or a dumb blonde. During the early and middle years of her career, of course, she did portray the archetypal dumb-blonde and seductive sex-siren and in many ways enjoyed the attention that these rôles attracted. But, far from dumb, she was quick to realise that this sort of attention was not enough to keep her satisfied, either in her career or in her personal life. She longed to be taken seriously as an actress and as a person – a desire which was expressed time and time again in her interviews. In the early stages of her career, when she was seeking the notice and acceptance of the highly critical 'Hollywood Circus', she played the part and kept the gossip columns and newspapers quoting silly and contrived comments. In Marilyn's case it was clever to be dumb. It was only after she was established as a major movie star and personality that she started to let people know her real feelings and motives. But even when she expressed her desire to approach 'serious' acting and took classes at The Actors Studio in New York City, her colleagues and contemporaries, along with the press, ridiculed her as pretentious. How could *Marilyn Monroe* ever seriously think she might tackle a role in *The Brothers Karamazov* – a lasting ambition she held – which required intelligence and high acting ability?

Marilyn Monroe had both. As I delved through mountains of interviews and press-cuttings, both in London and New York, this intelligence, combined with wit and sensitivity, became evident. Some quotes left me laughing at her sheer naïveté – but are they really so naïve?

ABOVE: MARILYN IN A SCENE
FROM 'SOMETHING'S GOTTA
GIVE', HER UNFINISHED
FINAL FILM.

Others left me with a very clear idea of the loneliness and despair she felt at having no love or warmth in her early life. But at no time is she just a dumb-blonde sex-symbol airing her views. These are the thoughts of a sensitive woman who cared about herself and the people around her.

Amongst the books about Marilyn are sincere and authentic accounts of experiences shared with her, more clinical accounts of her life from waif to superstar, and perhaps least attractive of all, sensationalist works relating unknown and perhaps untrue events. It was these latter books that made me set forth and compile the present volume. The famous who have died before they have had a chance to tell their own, complete stories, are perpetually at risk from those wishing to exploit a brief acquaintance or, more disturbing, to put words into their mouths. I don't claim to have spent forty days with her, to have directed any of her movies, or even to have swept her floors. I just thought it was time somebody gave Marilyn Monroe a chance. I thought it was about time Marilyn Monroe spoke for herself.

ROGER G. TAYLOR

ON CHILDHOOD

"NO KISSES OR PROMISES."

Since her mother was mentally unstable and considered an 'unfit' parent, and her father had left home before she was born, Marilyn spent the majority of her childhood in either orphanages or foster homes – a fact which was to have effect on her for the rest of her life.

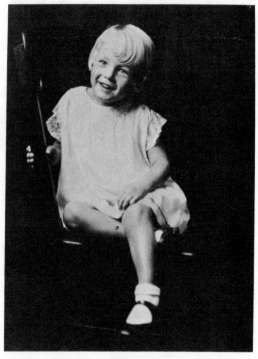

THE FIVE YEAR OLD MARILYN.

"Whenever I visited my mother I would stand looking at this photograph (of her father) and hold my breath for fear she would order me to stop looking. I had found out that people always ordered me to stop doing anything I liked to do."

"I used to be frightened when I visited her and spent most of my time in the closet of her bedroom hiding among her clothes."

"I don't remember seeing my father. I don't know what he looked like, I've been told he was a tall, thin man, good-looking with a moustache. I've never heard from him. I've been told he was killed in an automobile accident when I was six months old. My father is Abraham Lincoln – I mean I think of Lincoln as my father. He was wise and kind and good. He is my ideal, Lincoln, I love him."

"I used to make up daydreams, not about Mr. Gable, but about my father. When I'd be walking home from school in the rain and feeling bad I'd pretend my father was waiting for me, and that he would scold me for not having worn my rubbers. I didn't own any rubbers. Nor was the place I walked to any kind of a home. It was a place where I worked as a sort of child servant, washing dishes, clothes, floors, running errands and keeping quiet."

"I was never used to being happy, so that wasn't something I ever took for granted. You see, I was brought up differently from the average American child because the average child is brought up expecting to be happy – that's it, successful, happy and on time."

10

"Some of my foster families used to send me to the movies to get me out of the house and there I'd sit all day and way into the night – up in front, there with the screen so big, a little kid all alone, and I loved it. I loved anything that moved up there and I didn't miss anything that happened – and there was no popcorn either."

"No one ever told me I was pretty when I was a little girl. All little girls should be told they're pretty, even if they aren't."

'GIRL NEXT DOOR' PORTRAIT TAKEN BY BRUNO BERNARD.

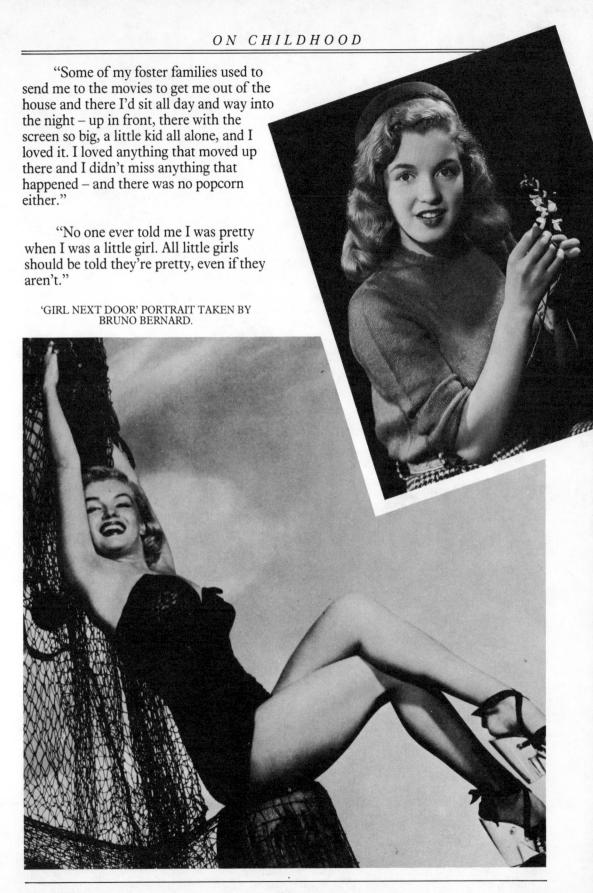

FROM A SERIES OF EXERCISE POSES.

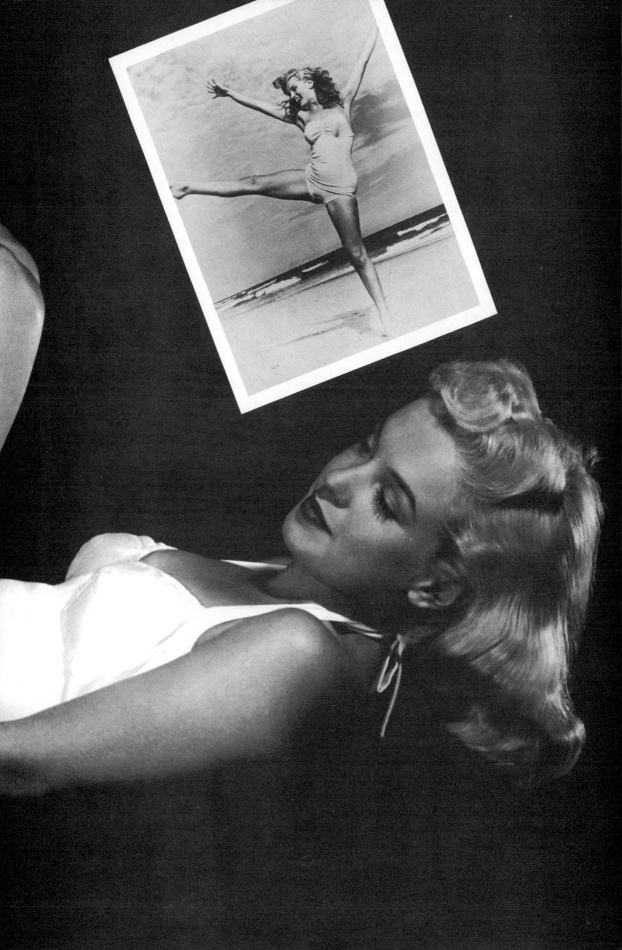

ABOVE AND RIGHT:
FILM STILLS FROM
'WE'RE NOT MARRIED'

"As I grew older I knew I was
different from other children because there
were no kisses or promises in my life. I
often felt lonely and wanted to die. I would
try to cheer myself up with daydreams.
I never dreamed of anyone loving me
as I saw other children loved. That was
too big a stretch for my imagination. I
compromised by dreaming of my attracting
someone's attention (besides God), of
having people look at me and say my
name."

"My impulse to appear naked and my dreams about it had no shame or sense of sin in them. Dreaming of people looking at me made me feel less lonely. I think I wanted them to see me naked because I was ashamed of the clothes I wore – the never-changing faded blue dress of poverty. Naked, I was like the other girls and not someone in an orphan's uniform."

"I dreamed of myself walking proudly in beautiful clothes and being admired by everyone and overhearing words of praise. I made up the praises and repeated them aloud as if someone else were saying them."

"Suddenly (aged 11) everything opened up. Even the girls paid a little attention to me just because they thought 'Hmm, she's to be dealt with'."

EARLY SEXY PICTURE TAKEN BY BRUNO BERNARD.

IN · HER · OWN · WORDS

ON FAME

"IN THE DISTANCE,
ACROSS THE SQUARE."

"The time when I sort of began to think I was famous I was driving somebody to the airport and as I came back there was this movie house and I saw my name in lights. I pulled the car up at a distance down the street – it was too much to take up close, you know – all of a sudden. And I said, 'God, somebody's made a mistake.' But there it was, in lights. And I sat there and said, 'So that's the way it looks,' and yet at the studio they had said, 'Remember you're not a star.' Yet there it is up in lights."

"I kept driving past the theater with my name on the marquee. 'Marilyn Monroe'. Was I excited. I wished they were using Norma Jean so that all the kids at the home and schools who never noticed me could see it."

"I really got the idea I must be a star, or *something*, from the newspapermen – I'm saying men, not the women – who would interview me and they would be warm and friendly. By the way, that part of the press, you know, the men of the press, unless they have their own personal quirks against me, they were always very warm and friendly and they'd say, 'You know, you're the only star,' and I'd say, 'Star?' and they'd look at me as if I were nuts. I think they, in their own kind of way, made me realize I was famous."

"In the morning the garbage men that go by 57th Street when I come out the door say, 'Marilyn, Hi! How do you feel this morning?' To me it's an honour and I love them for it. The working men – I'll go by and they'll whistle because they think, oh, it's a girl, she's got blonde hair and she's not out of shape, and then they say, 'Gosh, it's Marilyn Monroe,' and that has its . . . you know, those are the time it's nice, people knowing who you are and all of that, and feeling that you've meant something to them."

LEFT: RAY ANTHONY WROTE A SONG CALLED 'MARILYN'. HERE SHE PLAYS THE DRUMS FOR HIM.

LEFT: ENTERTAINING THE TROOPS IN KOREA 1952. ABOVE: SIR LAURENCE OLIVIER AND MARILYN AT THE SAVOY PRESS CONFERENCE TO ANNOUNCE MAKING OF 'THE PRINCE AND THE SHOWGIRL'. RIGHT: MARILYN ENJOYS A CIGGY!

"I think if other girls know how bad I was when I started they'll be encouraged. I finally made up my mind I wanted to be an actress and I was not going to let my lack of confidence ruin my chances."

"I feel as though it's all happening to someone right next to me. I'm close, I can feel it, I can hear it, but it isn't really me."

"It stirs up envy, fame does. People you run into feel that, well, who is she – who does she think she is, Marilyn Monroe? They feel fame gives them some kind of privilege to walk up to you and say anything to you, you know, of any kind of nature – and it won't hurt your feelings – like it's happening to your clothing."

ABOVE: MARILYN CHATS TO THE PRESS, OPPOSITE: MONROE AND MILLER.

"Usually they don't say it to me, they say it to the newspapers because that's a bigger play. You know, if they're only insulting me to my face that doesn't make a big enough play because all I have to do is say, 'See you around, like never.' But if it's the newspapers, it's coast to coast and on around the world. I don't understand why people aren't a little more generous with each other."

BELOW: WAITING TO GO BACK ON THE
SET, RIGHT: MARILYN WINS THE
1951 HENRIETTA AWARD AS
MOST PROMISING PERSONALITY
OF THE YEAR.

"But one thing about fame is the bigger people are or the simpler the people are, the more they are not awed by you. They don't feel they have to be offensive, they don't feel they have to insult you."

"The only trouble with becoming famous as a result of a half-dozen scandalous happenings is that the scandal-made star can't just rest on her old scandals. If she wants to keep her high place in the public eye and on the Hollywood producers' casting list she has to keep getting into more and more hot water. After you're thirty-five, getting into romantic hot water is a little difficult, and getting yourself publicized in love triangles and café duels over your favours needs not only smart press agents but also a little miracle to help out."

"I don't care about the critics. I don't care about anybody. The only people I care about are the people in Times Square, across the street from the theater, who can't get close as I come in. If I had light make-up on, they'd never see me. This make-up is for them, so that when I wave to them it will soften out in the distance across the square."

"But everybody is always tugging at you. They'd all like sort of a chunk of you. They kind of like take pieces out of you. I don't think they realize it, but it's like 'rrrr do this, rrrr do that . . .' but you do want to stay intact – intact and on two feet."

"Fame to me certainly is only a temporary and partial happiness – even for a waif. But fame is not really for a daily diet, that's not what fulfils you. It warms you a bit but the warming is temporary. It's like caviar but not when you have to have it every meal and every day."

"I now live in my work and in a few relationships with the few people I can really count on. Fame will go by and, 'So long, I've had you, fame.' If it goes by, I've always known it was fickle. So at least it's something I experienced, but that's not where I live."

LEFT: CUTTING THE FIRST ANNIVERSARY CAKE FOR CINEMA SCOPE. ABOVE: MARILYN HAVING HER HAIR SET 'GUILDA' FASHION BY HELEN HUNT FOR A HAIR SHOW GIVEN BY MS. HUNT. OPPOSITE: MARILYN GIVES HER EYEBROWS ONE LAST TOUCH BEFORE LEAVING FOR THE WORLD PREMIER OF 'HOW TO MARRY A MILLIONAIRE'.

ON SEX

"I'M VERY DEFINITELY
A WOMAN."

"Sex is a baffling thing when it doesn't happen. I used to wake up in the morning, when I was married, and wonder if the whole world was crazy, whooping about sex all the time. It was like hearing all the time that stove polish was the greatest invention on earth."

"Why I was a siren, I hadn't the faintest idea. There were no thoughts of sex in my head. I didn't want to be kissed, and I didn't dream of being seduced by a duke or a movie star. The truth was that with all my lipstick and mascara and precocious curves, I was as unsensual as a fossil. But I seemed to affect people quite otherwise."

"I wasn't aware of anything sexual in their new liking for me, and there were no sex thoughts in my mind. I didn't think of my body."

"People had a habit of looking at me as if I were some kind of mirror instead of a person. They didn't see me, they saw their own lewd thoughts, then they white-masked themselves by calling me the lewd one."

"People have curious attitudes about nudity, just as they have about sex. Nudity and sex are the most commonplace things in the world. Yet people often act as if they were things that existed only on Mars."

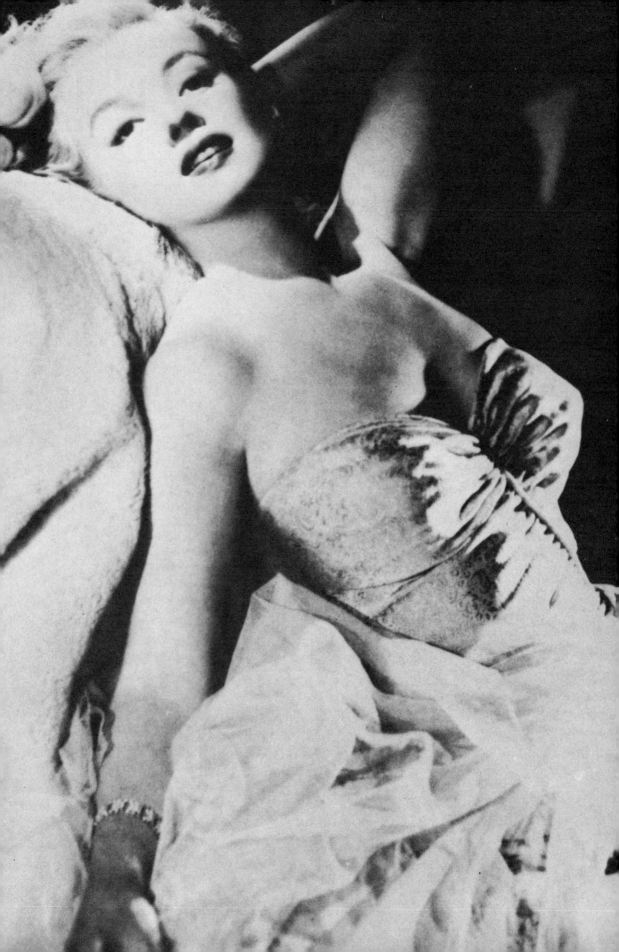

"I don't mind being burdened with being glamorous and sexual. But what goes with it can be a burden. I feel that beauty and feminity are ageless and can't be contrived, and glamour – although the manufacturers won't like this – cannot be manufactured. Not a real glamour, it's based on feminity. I think that sexuality is only attractive when it's natural and spontaneous. We are all born sexual creatures, thank God, but it's a pity so many people despise and crush this natural gift. Art, real art, comes from it – everything."

"Sex is part of nature. I go along with nature."

"It's easier to look sexy when you are thinking of one man in particular."

THIS PAGE AND OPPOSITE: A SCENE FROM 'SOMETHING'S GOT TO GIVE'.

"I have no prejudice against it (underwear)."

"What do I wear in bed? Why, Chanel No.5, of course."

Marilyn was asked if it was true that she only wore Chanel No.5 to bed:
"I like to wear something different once in a while. Now and then I switch to Arpège."

Asked how she kept her figure, Marilyn revealed:
"By eating spaghetti – and I do enjoy a good massage every so often."

After revealing a breast in a take for *The Misfits*:
"I love to do the things the censors won't pass. After all, what are we all here for? Just to stand around and let it pass us by?"

"Do I like to be photographed full face or profile? Profile every time when you have a beautiful profile all the way down."

"The trouble with censors is they worry if a girl has a cleavage. They ought to worry if she hasn't any."

Often asked if she wore falsies, Marilyn would usually retort ambiguously:
"Those who know me better, know better."

"Everything I have is my own."

During the filming of *The Misfits* Eli Wallach tried to upstage Marilyn by keeping her face turned away from the camera during a dance sequence. It did not cause her too much concern:
"The audience is going to find my rear more interesting than Eli's face anyhow."

Someone suggested that being 36 years of age might present problems:
"Thirty-six is just great when kids 12 to 17 still whistle."

And if the whistling ever stopped?:
"I'd probably just work at it harder."

"I'm very definitely a woman and I enjoy it."

"Men feel as if they want to spend *all* night with me."

Marilyn was asked if she thought that interest in sex was less predominant in England than Hollywood:
"I haven't taken a 'sexus' – I mean census – but sex is sex, and that's good isn't it?"

"How do I know about man's needs for a sex symbol? I'm a girl!!"

"My sin has been no more than I have written – posing for the nude picture because I needed fifty dollars desperately to get my automobile out of hock."

"No acting, just sex again. I had to wiggle across a room. I practised jiggling my backside for a week. Groucho loved it."

"I don't want to play sex rôles any more. I'm tired of being known as the girl with the shape."

"I never understood it – this sex symbol – I always thought symbols were things you clash together. That's the trouble, a sex symbol becomes a thing, I just hate being a thing. But if I'm going to be a symbol of something I'd rather have it sex than some other things we've got symbols of."

THE FAMOUS CALENDAR
SHOT WITH LACE
OVERPRINT.

OPPOSITE PAGE:
POSED SHOT FROM
'GENTLEMEN PREFER
BLONDES'.

ON LOVE AND MARRIAGE

"YOU CAN'T CURL UP
WITH A CAREER."

"I know it's considered chic for a husband and wife to have separate bedrooms, but I'm an old-fashioned girl who believes a husband and wife should share the same bedroom and bed."

On June 18th 1942, Norma Jean Baker married a young man named Jim Dougherty. It was just three weeks after her sixteenth birthday. The marriage was planned by her guardian, Grace Goddard. In 1946, while Dougherty was in Shanghai with the US Services, Norma Jean embarked on her modelling career, and he received notification of her wish to divorce. The marriage ended later that year. Of the marriage she said:

"Actually our marriage was a sort of friendship with sexual privileges. I found out later that marriages are often no more than that. And that husbands are chiefly good as lovers when they are betraying their wives."

In January 1954, Marilyn married American baseball star Joe DiMaggio. He found it very difficult to cope with being married to the famous and very public Marilyn Monroe. He became enraged during the filming of her most famous scene, standing over a subway grating with hot air blowing her skirt above her waist in *The Seven Year Itch* (1955). The marriage ended, but they remained close friends until her death. It is said he has not married since because of his unfailing love for her; at his request a single red rose is placed on her tomb every week:

"I had thought I was going to meet a loud sporty fellow. Instead I found myself smiling at a reserved gentleman in a gray suit, with a gray tie and a sprinkle of gray in his hair. There were a few blue polka dots in his tie. If I hadn't been told he was some sort of ball player, I would have guessed he was either a steel magnate or a congressman."

BELOW: JOE DIMAGGIO AND HIS
EX WIFE AT THE OPENING GAME
OF THE 1961 BASEBALL SEASON.
OPPOSITE: TAKEN AFTER MARILYN
ANNOUNCED HER SEPARATION
FROM MILLER.

They met on a blind date:

"We almost didn't meet. I'd heard of Joe DiMaggio but I didn't know much about him. I've never followed baseball . . . I was very tired the night of the date and asked if I could get out of it. But I'd promised. I had visualized him as having slicked back hair, wearing flashy sports clothes, with a New York line of patter . . . he had no line at all. No jokes. He was shy and reserved but, at the same time, rather warm and friendly. I noticed that he wasn't eating the food in front of him, that he was looking at me. Then the next thing I noticed was that I wasn't tired any more. Joe asked me to have dinner with him the next night. I had dinner with him that night, the next night, and every night until he had to leave for New York."

When Marilyn divorced Joe DiMaggio in late 1955, she said of the marriage:

"I had hoped for love, warmth and affection and understanding, but all I got was coolness and indifference."

"He didn't talk to me. He was cold. He was indifferent to me as a human being and an artist. He didn't want me to have friends of my own. He didn't want me to do my work. He watched television instead of talking to me."

In 1961 and 1962 Marilyn was seeing Joe DiMaggio again on a regular basis. She said:

"Thank God for Joe, thank God."

Monroe was asked if she was having an affair with American playwright, Arthur Miller:

"How could I – he's a married man."

ABOVE: MARILYN AND MILLER AFTER THEIR RELIGIOUS CEREMONY AT LEWISBORO, NEW YORK ON JULY 1, 1956, FOLLOWING THEIR CIVIL MARRIAGE.

"And on being asked what attracted her to Miller, she said:

"Everything, haven't you see him?"

After returning home from the party at which she first met Arthur Miller, she enthused:

"It was like running into a tree! You know, like a cool drink when you've got a fever. You see my toe – this toe? Well he sat and held my toe and we just looked into each other's eyes almost all evening."

In June 1956 Marilyn married Arthur Miller:

"He was going to make my life different – better, a lot better. If I were nothing but a dumb blonde, he wouldn't have married me."

"We're so congenial. This is the first time I think I've been really in love. Arthur is a serious man, but he has a wonderful sense of humour. We laugh and joke a lot. I'm mad about him."

"If Mr. Miller had a beard, he'd look like Lincoln."

"He has long legs that go on forever, and he only has two suits – the one he got married in and the other one."

"Movies are my business, but Arthur is my life."

"We live on the 13th floor in our apartment house, and that's exactly our attitude towards life."

"I'd like to do a play written by my husband. But he can't write – what do they say – vehicles. He can't write a part just for me. He writes subjects."

OPPOSITE: CHATTING DURING THE BREAK ON SET OF 'SOME LIKE IT HOT'. BELOW: MARILYN AND MILLER ON LOCATION NEAR RENO, NEVADA WHILE SHOOTING 'THE MISFITS'.

"He could have written me anything, and he comes up with this. If that's what he thinks of me, well, then, I'm not for him and he's not for me."

"All the time I was married to Arthur – four years – our life was set in a definite pattern. Summers in Connecticut – no deviation. Winters in our New York apartment. Then back to Connecticut."

"He is a wonderful writer, a brilliant man. But I think he is a better writer than a husband."

A reporter asked Marilyn to comment on Mas Lerner's remarks that Arthur Miller had sought out Marilyn because "he sensed he had come to an end in his writing". Before answering she insisted that the reporter promise to print her comment in its entirety. He agreed, and she replied:

"No comment."

Marilyn badly wanted to have children, but suffered more than one miscarriage. She was asked about her stepchildren Robert and Jane Ellen Miller, and Joe DiMaggio Jnr:

"I take a lot of pride in them, because they're from broken homes. I can't explain it but I think I understand about them. I think I love them more than I love anyone. I've always said to my stepchildren that I didn't want to be their mother – or stepmother – as such. I wanted to be their friend. Only time could prove that to them and they had to give me time. But I love them and I adore them. Their lives that are forming are very precious to me. And I know that I had a part in forming them."

"My career will have to work into my marriage or I'll do without my career. After all, a career is wonderful, but you can't curl up with a career on a cold night."

ABOVE: DIRECTOR JOHN HUSTON WITH MARILYN AND MILLER DURING PRODUCTION OF 'THE MISFITS'. OPPOSITE: MARILYN AND MILLER LAUGH WITH JACK LEMON WHILE MAKING 'SOME LIKE IT HOT'.

ON MEN

"HE'S SO SEXY, WOW!"

"The chief drawback with men is that they are too talkative. I don't mean intellectual men who are full of ideas and information about life. It's always a delight to hear such men talk because they are not talking boastfully. The over-talkative men who bore me are the ones who talk about themselves. Sometimes they confine themselves to plain uninterrupted boasting. They'll sit for an hour telling you how smart they are and how stupid everybody else around them is. Sometimes they don't even boast but give you an inside on what they like to eat and where they've been in the last five years."

"The most unsatisfactory men are those who pride themselves on their virility and regard sex as if it were some form of athletics at which you win cups. It is a woman's spirit and mood a man has to stimulate in order to make sex interesting. The real lover is the man who can thrill you by just touching your head or smiling into your eyes or by just staring into space."

On José Bolanos, her last lover:
"I hear he makes the worst movies in Mexico – but what do I care? Everything else he does is incredible."

And Laurence Olivier, with whom she shared a less than happy working relationship during the filming of *The Prince and the Showgirl*:
"He gave me the dirtiest looks, even when he was smiling!"

"There's another sort of man I've never liked – the sort that's afraid of insulting you. They always end up by insulting you worse than anybody. I much prefer a man to be a wolf and, if he has decided to make a pass at me, to make it and have it over with."

On Johnny Hyde, who was one of the first agents to take an active interest in her, both romantically and in her career. He was instrumental in her winning her first major acting rôle in *The Asphalt Jungle* but died before she reached the peak of her career:
"Johnny Hyde gave me more than his kindness and love. He was the first man I had ever known who understood me. Most men (and women) thought I was scheming and two-faced. No matter how truthfully I spoke to them or how honestly I behaved, they always believed I was trying to fool them."

OPPOSITE: MARILYN
AND OLIVIER.

"I like animals. If you talk to a dog or a cat it doesn't tell you to shut up."

On John Huston who directed Monroe in two of her movies, *The Asphalt Jungle* in 1950 and *The Misfits* in 1961. She greatly respected Huston but gradually began to mistrust directors in general after bad experiences with Billy Wilder and Otto Preminger:

"Mr. Huston was an exciting looking man. He was tall, long-faced, and his hair was mussed. He interrupted everybody with outbursts of laughter as if he were drunk. But he wasn't drunk. He was just happy for some mysterious reason, and he was also a genius – the first I had ever met."

When she was shown a photograph of John Huston embracing her she commented:

"Save this picture – I want to have it to show around when he begins saying things about me."

Also of Huston:

"He treats me like an idiot – 'Honey, this' and 'Honey, that'."

"It's a nice sensation to please an audience. I sat in the theater with Johnny Hyde. He held my hand. We didn't say anything on the way home. He sat in my room beaming at me. It was as if *he* had made good on the screen, not me. It was not only because I was his client and his 'discovery'. His heart was happy for me. I could feel his unselfishness and his deep kindness. He not only knew me, he knew Norma Jean, too. He knew all the pain and all the desperate things in me. When he put his arms around me and said he loved me, I knew it was true. Nobody had ever loved me like that. I wished with all my heart that I could love him back."

Frank Sinatra shared a close but short-lived relationship with Monroe:

"I can't tie him down, not Frankie, but I'll always love him."

She had admired Clark Gable since her childhood, believing that her father looked like him, sporting the same thin-line moustache. She won Mr. Gable's love and respect while filming *The Misfits* with him in 1961 and said of the actor:

"He never got angry with me once for blowing a line or being late or anything – he was a gentleman. The best."

"The place was full of so-called men, but Clark was the one who brought a chair for me between the takes."

"I could never be attracted to a man who had perfect teeth. A man with perfect teeth always alienated me. I don't know what it is but it has something to do with the kind of men I have known with perfect teeth. They weren't so perfect elsewhere."

On Montgomery Clift, her co-star in *The Misfits*:

"He's the only person I know who's in a worse shape than I am."

Her assessment of Billy Wilder, director of *Some Like it Hot*, was not enthusiastic:

"He's not a director, he's a dictator."

CLARK GABLE DANCES WITH
MARILYN AT A NIGHTCLUB.

OPPOSITE: MARILYN
DANCING WITH CLOSE
FRIEND JOHNNY HYDE
AT THE START OF
HER CAREER.

POSED SHOT FROM 'THE MISFITS':
MARILYN WITH MONTGOMERY CLIFT.

TOP: SET OF 'LET'S MAKE LOVE' WITH DIRECTOR
GEORGE CUKOR AND CO-STAR YVES MONTAND.
ABOVE: MILLER, SIGNORET, MONTAND, MARILYN
AND FRANKIE VAUGHN.

For seven years, commencing in the summer of 1948, Natasha Lytess was employed as Marilyn's acting coach, often creating tension and bad feeling with directors through her presence and interference on the film sets. Of Lytess she said:

"She was a great teacher, but she got really jealous about the men I saw. She thought she was my husband!"

"Men who think that a woman's past love affairs lessen her love for them are usually stupid and weak. A woman can bring a new love to each man she loves, providing there are not too many."

During the filming of *Let's Make Love* it is reputed that Marilyn had a short-lived love affair with her leading man, French actor Yves Montand:

"I love his voice, he's so sexy. Wow!"

"Next to my husband and along with Marlon Brando, Yves Montand is the most attractive man I've ever met."

MARILYN AND LAST PUBLIC ESCORT
ATTEND AN AWARD DINNER.

"The truth is I've never fooled anyone. I've let men sometimes fool themselves. Men sometimes didn't bother to find out who and what I was. Instead they would invent a character for me. I wouldn't argue with them. They were obviously loving somebody I wasn't. When they found this out, they would blame me for disillusioning them – and fooling them."

"The reality is very different – it's better to be unhappy alone than unhappy with someone – so far."

Marilyn Monroe was once asked what she didn't like about men:

"Nothing that I can think of."

LEFT: MARILYN WITH
DALE ROBERTSON. BELOW: MARILYN
AND MILTON GREEN NIGHTCLUBBING.
OPPOSITE: MARILYN AND COLUMNIST
SIDNEY SKOLSKY WHO WAS ALWAYS
ONE OF HER MOST LOYAL
SUPPORTERS AND FRIENDS.

IN · HER · OWN · WORDS

ON ACTING

"THE ONLY GROUND
I'VE EVER HAD TO STAND ON."

"Acting was something golden and beautiful. It wasn't an art. It was like a game you played that enabled you to step out of the dull world you knew into worlds so bright they made your heart leap just to think of them."

"You don't have to know anything to dream hard. I knew nothing about acting. I had never read a book about it, or tried to do it, or discussed it with anyone. I was ashamed to tell the few people I knew of what I was dreaming."

"I think I have one talent, I think it's observing. I hope that it adds up to acting. I hope to put it to good use."

"I felt sick. I had told myself a million times that I was an actress. I had practised acting for years. Here, finally was my first chance at a real acting part with a great director to direct me. And all I could do is stand with quivering knees and a quivering stomach and nod my head like a wooden toy."

"There were dozens of us on the set, bit players, with a gesture to make and a line or two to recite. Some of them were veteran bit players. After ten years in the movies they were still saying one line and walking ten feet towards nowhere. A few were young and had nice bosoms but I knew they were different from me. They didn't have my illusions. My illusions didn't have anything to do with being a fine actress. I knew how third-rate I was. I could actually feel my lack of talent, as if it were cheap clothes I was wearing inside. But, my God, how I wanted to learn, to change, to improve! I didn't want anything else. Not men, not money, not love, but the ability to act. With the arc lights on me and the camera pointed at me, I suddenly knew myself. How clumsy, empty, uncultured I was! A sullen orphan with a goose egg for a head."

ABOVE: STILL FROM
'HOW TO MARRY A MILLIONAIRE'.
OPPOSITE: MARILYN AND
RICHARD WIDMARK IN A SCENE FROM
'DON'T BOTHER TO KNOCK'.

TOP: FROM 'AS YOUNG AS YOU FEEL'.
ABOVE: STILL FROM 'WE'RE NOT MARRIED'.

A STILL FROM 'DON'T BOTHER TO KNOCK',
MADE IN 1952.

Auditioning for *Love Happy*:
  "There were three girls there and
Groucho had us each walk away from him.
I was the only one he asked to do it twice.
Then he whispered in my ear, 'You have
the prettiest ass in the business.' I'm sure
he meant it in the nicest way."

SET OF 'LET`S MAKE LOVE'.

"A struggle with shyness is in every actor more than anyone can imagine. There is a censor inside us that says to what degree we let go, like a child playing. I guess people think we just go out there, and you know, that's all we do – just do it. But it's a real struggle. I'm one of the world's most self-conscious people. I really have to struggle."

While filming *Some Like It Hot* Tony Curtis became infuriated with Marilyn's lateness on the set and her inability to remember her lines. He became increasingly bitter and said of one particular love scene that kissing Marilyn Monroe was like kissing Hitler, to which she replied:

"He only said that because I wore prettier dresses than he did."

"You've read there was some actor that once said about me that kissing me was like kissing Hitler. Well, I think that's *his* problem. If I have to do intimate love scenes with somebody who really has these kind of feelings toward me, then my fantasy can come into play. In other words, out with him, in with my fantasy. He was never there."

BELOW: MARILYN WITH ALBERT DEKKER IN 'AS YOUNG AS YOU FEEL'. OPPOSITE: MARILYN AND CO-STAR TONY CURTIS AT A COCKTAIL PARTY FOR 'SOME LIKE IT HOT'.

LEFT: MARILYN AS CHERIE IN
'BUS STOP'. ABOVE: MARILYN AND
JUNE HAVER IN 'LOVE NEST'.
OPPOSITE: STILL FROM
'DON'T BOTHER TO KNOCK'.

"I enjoy acting when you really hit it right. And I guess I've always had too much fantasy to be only a housewife. Well, also, I had to eat. I was never kept, to be blunt about it. I always kept myself. I have always had a pride in the fact that I was on my own."

"As a person my work is important to me. My work is the only ground I've ever had to stand on. Acting is very important. To put it bluntly I seem to have a whole super-structure with no foundation, but I'm working on the foundation."

"I'm looking forward to eventually becoming a marvellous – excuse the word marvellous – character actress. Like Marie Dressler, like Will Rogers. I think they've left this kind of appeal out of the movies today."

"All I want is to play something different – the Strasbergs say I can."

TOP: STILL FROM 'MONKEY BUSINESS' WITH CARY GRANT AND
CHARLES COBURN. INSET: STILL FROM 'THERE'S NO BUSINESS
LIKE SHOW BUSINESS' WITH DONALD O'CONNER.
ABOVE: MARILYN AND MILLER CHAT OFF SET.

'HOW WOULD YOU FEEL IF
SOMETHING OF YOURS BROKE IN
FRONT OF A WHOLE ROOM
FULL OF STRANGERS'.

"I never said I wanted to be a heavy tragic actress, or shun sexy parts. Besides, the feminine lead in Karamazov *is* a sexy role."

Marilyn was tackled by a reporter about her desire to play *The Brothers Grushenka*:

"I don't want to play the Brothers, I want to play Grushenka; that's a girl's part."

And when asked how to spell 'Grushenka':

"Well it starts with a 'G'."

"In many respects I'd like to become more mature. But that takes time, and you've got to work at it steadily. Most of all I'd like to be organised well enough so that I could accomplish everything that can possibly do. I want to be the best actress I can be."

BELOW: MARILYN HAS HER LEGS
MADE UP FOR 'LOVE NEST'.
RIGHT: STILL FROM 'DON'T BOTHER
TO KNOCK'. MARILYN AND
LURNE TUTTLE.

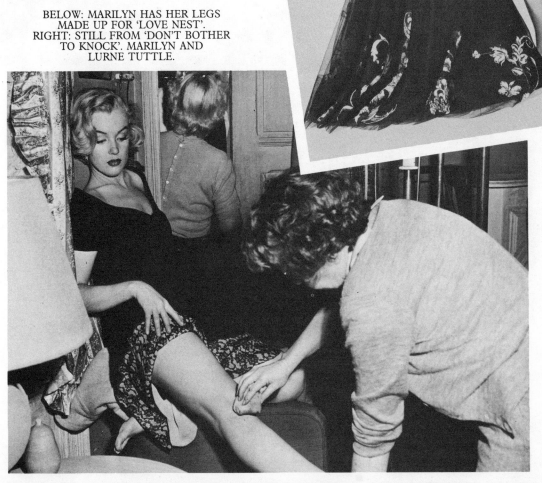

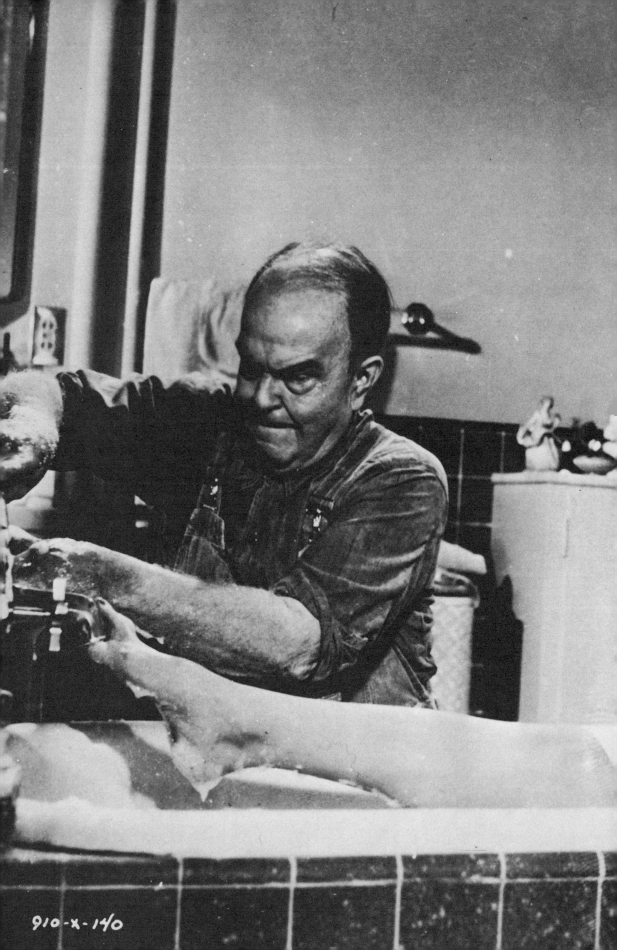

910-X-140

STILL FROM 'THE SEVEN YEAR ITCH'.

"I'm trying to find myself as a person, sometimes that's not easy to do. Millions of people live their entire lives without finding themselves. But it is something I must do. The best way for me to find myself as a person is to prove to myself that I'm an actress."

She was challenged with the question of what she would do if 50 per cent of the experts in Hollywood said she had no talent and should give up:

"Look, if 100 per cent told me that, all 100 per cent would be wrong. That's why I'm studying acting and music. I believe if I make myself the best actress there is, I have to reach the top."

BELOW: STILL FROM 'SOMETHING'S GOT TO GIVE'.

ON STARDOM AND THE SYSTEM

"WHATEVER I AM,
I AM THE BLONDE!"

"And I want to say that the people – if I am a star – the people made me a star; no studio, no person, but the people did . . . When they all rushed toward me I looked behind me to see who was there and I said, 'My Heavens!' I was scared to death. I used to get the feeling, and sometimes I still get it, that sometimes I was fooling somebody."

When Marilyn obtained her first major film contract she was heard to say:

"Well, that's the last cock *I* have to suck."

"Success came to me in a rush. It surprised my employers much more than it did me. Even when I had played only bit parts in a few films, all the movie magazines and newspapers started printing my picture and giving me write-ups. I used to tell lies in my interviews – chiefly about my mother and father. I'd say she was dead and he was somewhere in Europe. I lied because I was ashamed to have the world know my mother was in a mental institution – and that I had been born 'out of wedlock' and never heard my illegal father's voice."

"If I'd observed all the rules, I'd never have got anywhere."

"Everybody in the studio wanted me as a star in his movie. I finally went into *Gentlemen Prefer Blondes*, and after that, *How to Marry a Millionaire*. I liked doing these pictures. I liked the fact that I was important in making them a great financial success and that my studio cleaned up a fortune, despite the fact that its chiefs had considered me unphotogenic. I liked the fact that the movie salesmen who came to Hollywood for a big studio sales rally whistled loudest and longest when I entered their midst."

"I remember when I got the part in *Gentlemen Prefer Blondes*, Jane Russell – she was the brunette in it and I was the blonde – she got $200,000 for it and I got my $500 a week, but that to me was, you know, considerable. She, by the way, was quite wonderful to me. The only thing was I couldn't get a dressing room. I said, finally – I really got to this kind of level – I said,

OPPOSITE:
A CLASSIC PUBLICITY STILL.

'Look, after all, I *am* the blonde and it *is Gentlemen Prefer Blondes!*' Because still they kept saying, 'Remember, you're not a star'. I said, 'Well, whatever I am, I *am* the blonde!' "

On Jane Russell:

"We got along nicely – Jane called me the 'round one' – I don't know what she means by that, but I assume she means it to be friendly."

BOTTOM: STILL FROM 'GENTLEMEN PREFER BLONDES'. BELOW: MARILYN AND JANE RUSSELL POSE FOR FANS. OPPOSITE: STILL FROM 'GENTLEMEN PREFER BLONDES'.

ON LOCATION FROM 'THE MISFITS'.
MARILYN CHATS TO FOUR YEAR
OLD DAUGHTER OF CREW MEMBER.

"My travels have always been of the same kind. No matter where I've gone or why I've gone there it ends up that I never see anything. Becoming a movie star is living on a merry-go-round. When you travel you take the merry-go-round with you. You don't see natives or new scenery. You see chiefly the same press agents, the same sort of interviewers and the same picture layouts of yourself."

While Marilyn was in the process of filming *The Misfits* she said of Arthur Miller (her husband, and writer of the film) and John Huston (the director):

"It's their movie. It's really about the cowboys and the horses. That's all they need. They don't need me at all. Not to act – just for the money. To put my name on the marquee."

MARILYN IN 'LET'S MAKE LOVE'.

STILL FROM 'ALL ABOUT EVE'.

And of directors in general:

"You feel they're more interested in their directing than they are in your acting. They want the front office to praise *them* when the rushes are shown. Mr. Huston wasn't like that. He was interested in the acting I did. He not only watched it, he was part of it. And even though my part was a minor one, I felt as if I were the most important performer in the picture – when I was before the camera. This was because everything I did was important to the director, just as important as everything the stars of the picture did."

"Only the public can make a star – it's the studios who try to make a system out of it."

rilyn MONROE · Joseph COTTEN · Jean PETERS

Casey ADAMS · Denis O'DEA · Richard ALLAN · Don WILSON · Lurene TUTTLE
Russell COLLINS · Will WRIGHT

ackett, Walter Reisch and Richard Breen

will be used for exhibition purposes and NOT for resale

Directed by Henry HATHAWAY

Copyright 20th Century-Fox Film Co., Ltd

Marilyn Monroe had a constant fear of becoming mentally unbalanced, as her mother had. She urged Bill Travilla, her dress designer at the time:

"Promise me one thing, Billy, if it ever happens to me, you come over and get me and don't let people see me. Just hide me somewhere."

Of her fear of being misrepresented by the press she remarked:

"I might never see that article and it might be okayed by somebody in the studio. This is wrong because when I was a little girl I read signed stories in fan magazines and I believed every word the stars said in them. Then I'd try to model my life after the lives of the stars I read about. If I'm going to have that kind of influence, I want to be sure it's because of something I've actually read or written."

DAN MURRAY AND MARILYN IN
SCENES FROM 'BUS STOP'.

"I realized that just as I had once fought to get into the movies and become an actress, I would now have to fight to become myself and to be able to use my talents. If I didn't fight I would become a piece of merchandise to be sold off the movie pushcart."

"It might be kind of a relief to be finished. It's sort of like I don't know what kind of a yard dash you're running, but then you're at the finish line and you sort of sigh – you've made it! But you never have – you have to start all over again."

"I used to say to myself, 'What the devil have you got to be proud about, Marilyn Monroe?' And I'd answer, 'Everything, everything,' and I'd walk slowly and turn my head slowly as if I were a queen."

IN · HER · OWN · WORDS

ON HOLLYWOOD

"JUST A PLACE TO WORK IN."

"In Hollywood a girl's virtue is much less important than her hair-do. You're judged by how you look, not by what you are. Hollywood's a place where they'll pay you a thousand dollars for a kiss, and fifty cents for your soul. I know, because I turned down the first offer often enough and held out for the fifty cents."

"When I was younger, I used to go to Grauman's Chinese Theater and try to fit my foot in the prints in the cement there. And I'd say, 'Oh, oh, my foot's too big, I guess that's out.' I did have a funny feeling later when I finally put my foot down into that wet cement. I sure knew what it really meant to me – anything's possible, almost."

"If you've noticed in Hollywood where millions and billions of dollars have been made, there aren't any kind of monuments or museums – and I don't call putting your footprint in Grauman's Chinese Theater a monument – all right, this did mean a lot of sentimental ballyhoo to me at the time. Gee, nobody left anything behind, they took it, they grabbed it and they ran – the ones who made the billions of dollars, never the workers."

"Hollywood parties not only confuse me, but they often disillusion me. The disillusion comes when I meet a movie star I've been admiring since childhood."

"I always thought that movie stars were exciting and talented people, full of special personality. Meeting one of them at a party I discover usually that he (or she) is colorless and even frightened. I've often stood silent at a party for hours listening to my movie idols turn into dull and little people."

"The reason I went to parties of this sort was to advertise myself. There was always the possibility that someone might insult me or make a pass at me, which would be good publicity if it got into the

OPPOSITE: MARILYN WITH
CO-STAR ROBERT MITCHUM
IN 'RIVER OF NO RETURN'.
BELOW: MAGAZINE COVER
'MOVIELAND'.

movie columns. But even if nothing extra happened, just to be reported in the movie columns as having been present at a movie society gathering is very good publicity. Sometimes it is the only favorable mention the movie queens can get. There was also the consideration that if my studio bosses saw me standing among the regular movie stars they might get to thinking of me as a star also."

RIGHT: MARILYN WITH CARY GRANT, A STILL FROM 'MONKEY BUSINESS' DIRECTED BY HOWARD HAWKS. OPPOSITE: FANTASY SEQUENCE FROM 'THE SEVEN YEAR ITCH'.

After a Hollywood dinner honouring visiting Soviet Premier Khrushchev:

"I could tell Khrushchev liked me. He smiled more when he was introduced to me than for anyone else at the whole banquet. He squeezed my hand so long and hard I thought he would break it. I guess it was better than having to kiss him, though."

OPPOSITE: MARILYN HAVING HER FORTUNE TOLD BY A FAMOUS HOLLYWOOD FORTUNE TELLER.

"I don't know if high society is different in other cities, but in Hollywood important people can't stand to be invited some place that isn't full of other important people. They don't mind a few unfamous people being present because they make good listeners. But if a star or studio chief or any other great movie personages find themselves sitting among a lot of nobodies, they get frightened – as if somebody was trying to demote them."

MARILYN MEETS THE QUEEN 1956 ROYAL COMMAND PERFORMANCE.

"When you're a failure in Hollywood – that's like starving to death outside a banquet hall with the smells of *filet mignon* driving you crazy."

"New York is my home now. Hollywood is just a place to work in."

After reading a film script that had been proposed for a film *The Jean Harlow Story*, Marilyn commented:

"I hope they don't do that to me after I'm gone."

OPPOSITE: MARILYN ASTRIDE A
PINK ELEPHANT AT MADISON SQUARE
GARDEN 1955. BELOW: TAKING THE AIR.
LEFT: ARRIVING WITH MILLER TO
START FILMING
'PRINCE AND THE SHOWGIRL'.

ON BEING LATE

"IT'S REMARKABLE THAT
I GET THERE AT ALL."

"I have many bad social habits. People are always lecturing me about them. I am invariably late for appointments – sometimes as much as two hours. I've tried to change my ways but the things that make me late are too strong – and too pleasing."

"When I have to be somewhere for dinner at eight o'clock, I will lie in the bathtub for an hour or longer. Eight o'clock will come and go and I still remain in the tub. I keep pouring perfumes into the water and letting the water run out and refilling the tub with fresh water. I forget about eight o'clock and my dinner date. I I keep thinking and feeling far away."

"Sometimes I know the truth of what I'm doing. It isn't Marilyn Monroe in the tub but Norma Jean. I'm giving Norma Jean a treat. She used to have to bath in water used by six or eight other people. Now she can bath in water as clean and transparent as a pane of glass. And it seems that Norma can't get enough of fresh bath water that smells of real perfume."

"I guess people think that why I'm late is some kind of arrogance and I think it is the opposite of arrogance. I also feel that I'm not in this big American rush – you know, you got to go and you got to go fast but for no good reason. The main thing is, I do want to be prepared when I get there to give a good performance or whatever to the best of my ability."

"A lot of people can be there on time and do nothing, which I have seen them do, and you know, all sit around and sort of chit-chatting and talking trivia about their social life. Gable said about me, 'When she's there, she's there. All of her is there! She's there to work.'"

"It makes something in me happy to be late. People are waiting for me. People are eager to see me. I remember all the years I was unwanted, all the hundreds of times nobody wanted to see the little servant girl, Norma Jean – not even her mother. And I feel a queer sensation in punishing the people who are wanting me now. But it's not them I'm really punishing. It's the long-ago people who didn't want Norma Jean. The later I am, the happier she grows. To me, it's remarkable that I get there at all."

"I don't think I'm as late as I used to be, and once I arrived at a cocktail party on time and nobody was there. So what are you supposed to do – sit around? Of course it's a good way to get acquainted with the hostess – but usually the hostess isn't ready either. As long as I'm on time in the important areas, like making boats and

JACK LEMMON AND MARILYN ON THE
BEACH AT CANNES FILMING
'SOME LIKE IT HOT'.

planes or getting to the theater before the curtain goes up, it's all right with Arthur if I'm late to other places. He says he finds it isn't necessary to be on time for most things because you just have to stay there longer if you do."

During the filming of *Some Like It Hot* Marilyn was consistently late on the set, much to the annoyance and frustration of fellow actors Tony Curtis and Jack Lemmon and director Billy Wilder. A director's aide who was sent to inform her that she was very late and that other actors were waiting for her was told:

"Go fuck yourself.'

OPPOSITE: BILLY WILDER EXPLAINS THE SKIRT BLOWING SCENE FROM 'THE SEVEN YEAR ITCH' TO MARILYN.

THE WIT OF MARILYN MONROE

"HE WON'T LET ME PLAY LINDBERGH."

"We did some test scenes of me in a pool, sort of nude. I hope they give me some good nude lines to go with it."

"I don't know why the US Marines in Korea laughed when I said 'sweater girls'? Take away their sweaters and what have you got?"

"When Dior announced his straight line fashion I said, 'If this comes about I shall be a dead duck'."

"I'm not only proud of my firm bosom but I'm going to be proud of my firm character."

"A sack allows you to move. And it moves with you. And movement is – well, movement is good."

"I do not like suntan because I like to feel blonde all over."

Her comment on her 'baby stare' was direct:

"That's because of the parts I play. If I play a stupid girl and ask a stupid question I've got to follow it through. What am I supposed to do – look intelligent?"

"I sit down the way I feel. I learned to walk as a baby and I haven't had a lesson since. I use walking to get around."

"I always sleep with my mouth open. I know because it's open when I wake up."

At one stage in her life Monroe was placed in a ward for 'Highly Disturbed Patients' in the Payne Whitney Psychiatric Clinic in New York City. As she left she said:

"Just before I left, I told all those

doctors they should have their heads examined."

And whilst still there she quipped:
"Payne Whitney gives me a pain."

"When I talk I have a habit of not finishing sentences, and this gives the impression I'm telling lies. I'm not. I'm just not finishing sentences."

In 1949 Marilyn posed in the nude for a calendar shot by photographer Tom Kelley. In later years, when she had become an established film actress, it was discovered that 'Miss Golden Dreams' was in fact the now-famous Monroe. Consequently the calendar sold millions and helped establish Marilyn Monroe as everybody's favourite pin-up and movie star. She was asked why she did it:
"Hunger."

And what she had on:
"The radio."

"I know *I* would go and see a movie starring Sir Laurence Olivier and Marilyn Monroe – the casting is so, how do you say it, incongruous."

"Billy Wilder's a wonderful director. I want him to direct me again. But he's doing *The Lindbergh Story* next. And he won't let me play Lindbergh."

"I'm not interested in money – I just want to be wonderful."

When Marilyn returned to America after filming *The Prince and the Showgirl* with Laurence Olivier she was asked to comment on the difference between British fans and reporters and those in America. She observed:
"The only difference is that over there everybody is English."

Once asked if she had any love interests, she offered:
"No, no serious interests – but I'm always interested."

And sometimes she was even stirred into verse:
"Here goes –
Good night
Sleep tight
And sweet repose
Wherever you lay your head
I hope you find your nose."

ABOVE: VIVIEN LEIGH AND LAURENCE OLIVIER SAY GOODBYE TO MARILYN AND MILLER AFTER SHOOTING 'THE PRINCE AND THE SHOWGIRL'. OPPOSITE: OLIVIER AND MARILYN.

END PIECE

"Please don't make me a joke. End the interview with what I believe – I don't mind making jokes but I don't want to look like one."

Monroe was asked if it worried her that she was thought of as dumb:

"Things go on in my mind that no-one knows about! I've always figured things out and done them according to plan. Oh no – I'm not calculating or tricky. But I know what I want."

"Someday I want to have a home of my own with trees and grass and hedges all around, but never trim them at all – just let them grow any old way they want."

And when asked if she would do anything differently if she had the chance to do it again, Marilyn replied:

"I think I'd do everything differently. I'd make every single decision differently – except I don't think I'd have found what I've found now, at last. So if all of it was necessary for me to reach this point, and it seems that it was, then it was worth it."

AMERICA'S GREATEST MOVIE MAGAZINE

modern screen

DELL MAGAZINE MAR 20¢

Sidney Skolsky: THE LOWDOWN ON HOLLYWOOD WOMEN

Marilyn Monroe

MARILYN'S CASKET IS BORNE FROM
THE CHAPEL TO THE CRYPT.
IN THE PROCESSION FROM THE
CHAPEL TO CRYPT – JOE DIMAGGIO
AND HIS SON JOE JR.